G000135239

More than bananas

Fizz books

www.fizz-books.com

More than bananas

*How the Christian faith works for me and
for the whole Universe*

Glenn Myers

Copyright © 2014 Glenn Myers

First published 2014 by Fizz Books

Fizz Books Ltd
Suite 34, 67-68 Hatton Garden, London EC1N 8JY
www.fizz-books.com

ISBN 978-0-9565010-5-9 (paperback)
ISBN 978-0-9565010-6-6 (epub)

3

Cover design by Chris Lawrence

redsq_design@yahoo.co.uk

British Library Cataloguing in Publication Data

A CIP catalogue for this book is available from the British
Library

Printed by Lightning Source UK Ltd, Chapter House, Pitfield,
Kiln Farm, Milton Keynes MK11 3LW UK
Printed on paper from managed, sustainable forests, certified by
the FSC (UK books) and the SFI (US books)

for my son Thomas,
of whom I am inordinately proud.

CONTENTS

INTRODUCTION

I wrote this book between mid-August and mid-October 2013, after a strange period in my life when doctors saved my life on three separate occasions in four years. I have never written an easier book. I think it was because I'd been thinking and blogging about this stuff for a long time.

It describes how the Christian faith works for me, and in my view, for the whole Universe. The title comes from my belief that current science, almost magical as it is in explaining lots of things, doesn't quite do it as an explanation of who we are really. It gives a fine account of why I eat bananas; it's less good on why I puzzle about how to live a meaningful life.

Hope you enjoy the book. Feel free to email if you'd like to continue the discussion. I hope to put some of the questions and responses up on a website somewhere if that's OK.

Glenn Myers, Cambridge, October 2013

www.glennmyers.info

1 THE PROBLEM

It's odd that we exist at all. Yet we usually ignore this because:

1. It's really too hard to think about

and

2. We have many other problems that take our attention. Here are some of mine (I am on holiday). *Was that a grey hair I saw this morning? Is it too chilly to sit outside? Can I be bothered to make another cup of coffee before lunch?*

Yet perhaps we ought to try to think about the big stuff, at least once in our lives. Today I am writing this, looking out over Pembrokeshire hills. Today (a different today) you are reading what I have written. We are linked across time by a thread of text and thought. The fact we are each thinking thoughts is perhaps evidence enough that you and I both exist.

How can we exist?

We have no idea how or why this happened, or what to do about it. Instead of nothingness, there's us. Instead of a blank oblivion, there are celebrity TV shows, duck-billed platypuses, galaxies, music, cheese, and you and I.

There's got to be a story behind this. How was this allowed to happen? How did nothing become something? And how did the something become this?

Science takes us part of the way, a dazzling story, now well known in outline: the start of the Universe in a burst of light; the development of complex atoms; a happy, random arrangement of organic molecules that leads to the self-replicating machine called Life; mistakes in the self-replicating machine which means it can develop new forms; then squillions of years of adaption and growth and finally some hairy beasts wandering the African savannah in search of soft fruit.

My problem is that all this wonderful scheme only explains a little bit of us. It accounts for my liking for bananas and sex, because both those things help preserve my genes for the next generation. It means I'm pretty darn good at shopping, especially down the fruit aisle, where intelligence matters for nutrition. You won't find me mistaking an avocado for a mango. In all this, I am evolution's child.

But why do I hope and dream? Why do I hum music? Why do I long to meet God? Why does death, so normal a part of the cosmic order, as necessary as compost, feel like a rip in my personal space-time? Why do I love?

How come, when the evolutionary tree separated, one branch became an orang-utang but the other started to write poetry? What happened to us that we became so extraordinarily different? We yearn to scratch our bums along with the whole itchy-bottomed creation, but only we resist the urge because we are self-conscious about it. Where did all this self-consciousness come from? Why are we so alike, and yet so unlike, our evolutionary first cousins?

It must be that evolution is only half an answer, and it is the boring half. All the colour and variety of the evolved world are just re-jigged kaleidoscope patterns compared with the astonishing fact of our consciousness, our yearnings, our humanity.

That pushes me to thinking that Someone had a hand in creating me and you, someone with spunk and personality. Mere evolution is chemical, mechanical, digital. It is also humourless and soulless. I am not that way, and neither are you. I may be 70% water, but I am more than just a well-hydrated *bouquet garni*.

A Creator

So we are suggesting a Someone who created me. Let me, in a naughty thrill of political incorrectness, call that Someone a him.

I have no reason to do this beyond a desire not to get sidetracked. If a Creator is going to create he must contain within himself every possibility of maleness and femaleness and much else beside. So we can't call him 'him' (since it excludes his herness) or 'her' (for the equal and opposite reason). Yet to call this Someone an 'it' seems rude. An 'it' is less than human, not more. So since the thought-police are better at destroying language than improving it, and haven't left us with a decent alternative, I'm going to call this Someone a him, get it over with, and move on.

If we suggest a Creator, we may as well let him create the whole lot. Let's, in other words, have a proper Creator, one who starts with nothing except himself and creates everything, without help.

A moment of creation

Annoyingly for many people, this view sits well with current science. Everything points back to a Big Bang, a moment of creation, less than 14 billion years ago.

I am old enough to remember that this theory used to be controversial. We used to have two theories about origins, a continuous creation (or Steady State) model and the Big Bang model. The Big Bang model had much against it. It was dreamed up by a cosmologist who had the bad taste to be a Catholic priest, and who could therefore be accused of re-introducing the idea of Creation via a scientific back door.

Deciphering the evidence for the Big Bang took lots of hard maths and a long investigation to decide whether a radio signal was really the dying echo of Creation's song or pigeon-droppings on the aerial, but eventually the accumulating evidence became overwhelming. The Steady State Theory wobbled and decayed into the nothingness from whence it arose, and the physicists trudged into line.

It is embarrassing for a physicist, but these things have to be faced. Some of the most brilliant theoretical and observational work through the 20th century led us round an unexpected corner and smack into the face of a Creator. Many physicists hope this intolerable Big Bang theory will not last. Perhaps it will not. Some work hard to overcome it. But it is orthodoxy for now.

So our picture is of a Creator who set off the cosmic fireworks in an insouciant and impenetrable display of cosmic brilliance. Then somewhere along the line, perhaps in a dribble, perhaps in a flash, he poured something of his own person-ness into the evolving dust. Part of creation became like him, inquisitive, creative, random, caring, free. The dry and barren Universe hosted souls. That picture goes somewhere towards explaining us: not as far as we'd like, but a start.

It also spawns a lot more questions, which the smallest child can ask, and the smartest adult cannot answer. Here are three:

1. If there is a Creator, where did he come from?

2. Why did he do what he did? Why does he do what he does?

and

3. Why is there both happiness and unhappiness in the world?

2 LET'S GET ONTOLOGICAL

I am going to suggest a Creator who is infinite in every direction.

This saves time. We could of course suggest a different kind of god, one more powerful than us but not going the whole God-hog. Such a being would be able to create us, perhaps, but he would leave the question open as to what greater being or what clever laws created *him*. It becomes like the kids' game of 'name the biggest number you can':

'Four million'

'Four hundred million'

'Four hundred million million million'

'Four hundred million million million squintillion'

'Squintillion isn't a number!'

'Yes it is! I saw it in a book!'

'All right. Four hundred million million million squintillion and one'

(Pause for a fight)

We may as well just escalate everything to infinity and eternity and see what the view is like when we do this.

Eternal...

Let's first imagine a God who is eternal. Now eternity isn't just a very long time, like when you are waiting for your wife to get ready, or when you are listening to a boring person who says 'errm' aggressively to hold the floor while they marshall more boring things in their boring head to bore you with. Either of these can feel like eternity but they are not the real thing.

To be eternal is to be beyond the reach of time, but to be really eternal and really God is to be able to reach into time also. Before the earth and the world, before the mountains rose and sunk, further back than the Big Bang, forever God; yet also able to reach into the world of cause and effect and stir it like sugar in coffee. A God untrammelled, timeless and timely, the Time Lord.

Such an eternal God must see things differently from those of us who are restricted to the good ship *Here-and-Now*, tugged along the current of time.

For one thing, he must see the big picture. The whole story of our Universe, and the origin and destiny of humanity, must be spread out before him like a rumpled duvet.

Second, it must be hard, if you are an eternal being, to decide what is big and what is small. A moment, a millennium, an aeon are equally brushstrokes on the great canvas. A brief friendship between you and the Almighty may be as important to him as the whole history of the Chinese Empire or the age of the dinosaurs. It's hard to separate things into their relative importance because they are all exquisitely necessary parts of the whole.

Take the gold ring on my finger as an example. Physics tells us gold is made when giant stars explode. Then over billions of years gold dust spreads across the Universe. Finally it coalesces into being a part of Planet Earth, perhaps that part of Planet Earth that is found in a mine in South Africa. This gold is dug up and becomes my wedding ring. Perhaps when I die it lies with me again in the soft earth until the sun becomes a Red Giant and melts the earth and returns the gold to the interstellar void.

From the view of an eternal being, how do you tell the story of that gold? Is its real story the billions of years in space, in a Universe that wears out? Or is its story its brief moment as a symbol of human love, that lasts only decades in the Universe but, being love, remains when the Universe fades to black? What counts to an eternal being? Who knows, but it's probably different from what counts to us.

Third, and most bizarrely, cause and effect must look different when viewed from eternity. Perhaps things that are viewed in time as happening later than other things are revealed in eternity as essentially entangled all along. When two events have a foothold in the timeless, effect and cause dissolve into mush.

As we will see later in the book, I find these ideas are important in providing a faith that is strong and elastic enough to do its job.

Infinite...

But the God we are suggesting is not just eternal. He is also infinite. He is infinitely good at everything he is and does and he is also infinitely good, when necessary, at hiding how infinitely good he is.

If God is infinitely wise, we, who see a little bit, might grasp the outermost layers of his wisdom. Science does some of that, thinking God's thoughts after him. So do our hearts, perhaps especially when someone gets what we think they deserve.

But what about when they don't get what they deserve? If God's wisdom is infinite it must extend beyond our capacity to trace it out. Some of God's wisdom must look like foolishness to us. It does not look that way to God, because he is wise all the way down. God is so wise he can ask questions of himself that only he can understand and answer. He can solve puzzles that only he can think up.

The same goes for all his qualities. God is good all the way down, even though we limited humans see evil at work in the world. God is all-powerful, which must mean everything that happens is in some sense his fault. Yet God is (infinitely) able to set his creation free to do what it likes: does that mean everything isn't his fault after all? Or can you perfectly abdicate your responsibilities while also perfectly retaining them? (For answers refer, above, to the infinite Wisdom of God.)

God is infinitely kind, even if he doesn't seem that way to us; infinitely compassionate even though the world seems cruel; infinitely old and infinitely fresh and young and curious. He must be infinitely alone and infinitely companionable, infinitely solitary and utterly gregarious. He must be infinitely streetwise and infinitely naive. He must be unflinching and eternal in his hatred of injustice; and also infinite in his tenderness both to abused and abuser. He must have an infinitely good sense of humour, which explains much about this Universe, not least the New Atheist movement or the existence of three-toed sloths.[1]

God 1.0

We have taken all the best things we know, including personality itself, stretched them until they are eternal and infinite, and identified the result as 'God'. Or at least, 'our minimum, basic requirement for God'. There's surely more realms of God-ness that we have no capacity to grasp. But any God worth the name God must be at least this.

We still don't know how he got here and nor can we get far in understanding his behaviour.

---

[1] The sloth is the world's slowest mammal. It sleeps for 15-20 hours per day and even when awake can remain motionless for such long periods that algae starts to grow on it. You can find cruel YouTube videos of them crossing roads; but see them moving languidly through the trees and they are godlike, lithe and beautiful. International Sloth Day (I am not making this up) falls on October 20th each year—if anyone can be bothered to wake up for it.

I suggest that such a God at the heart of our contradictory, improbable Universe, behind our existence, behind our humanity, fits the facts better than any other theory. At least it does for me.

3 LOVE AND PAIN

That leads us to a second question. OK, infinitely wise, kind, powerful God, we have an issue here. Why is there so much pain in the world? And what are you doing about it?

God may be wise and loving all the way down. But pain is still pain, and so the question is still live.

I agree we also have to ask a parallel question: why is there also so much goodness, joy, grace and fun in the world? The two questions do go together. And asking them both at once has the happy side-effect of keeping us sane. If we only explored the Problem of Pain without thinking also about the Problem of Love it would make us as miserable as a Russian novelist or even as Thomas Hardy, *and* without their literary panache: *too* grim.

It's tedious and depressing to list the misery in the world. There's so much of it. I hardly want to start the list: children abused, dictators who run countries to fill their own wallets and won't let anyone else have a turn; injustice everywhere, cancer, loneliness and minor acts of meanness on the road against people driving innocent but unfashionable cars.

At the same time, inexplicable good often oozes from the wounds. Cut us down, still we hope, and we don't always know why. We grow back and rebuild and fight another day. Children still think *why walk when you can skip?* We dance, even us oldies. We play. Evil does its worst and we produce our best. We keep falling in with people who are nice and funny and good. They do kind things.

I watch the primary school children at the end of the school day, running to see their parents, arms wheeling. *Don't you know,* I ask, *that after Life has had you for a bit, some of you are going to be divorced, alcoholic, diseased, embittered? (Look at your parents if you don't believe me.) Why did you, why do you hope?* Their arms still wheel.

Very oddly, Creation itself mirrors this human experience. As I write, somewhere in the world, some teenage chimps are slowly torturing a bonobo monkey to death for fun. A frog is dying of thirst in my garden, perhaps calling fruitlessly to God for a lap of water to wash in or a juicy slug to eat. Above the frog, in the cherry tree, collared doves coo, apparently for no other reason than happiness at sitting on a tree branch in the sunshine.

On the holiday in Pembrokeshire from which we have now returned, our dog fetched thrown sticks from the ocean, coughing up water, eyes dreamy with joy. Creation too, in our eyes at least, is blithe and carefree and cruel and sad.

Oscar's insight

Oscar Wilde had something to say about this. Of course he played out in his own life the extremes of grace and pain. A Mozart with words, a literary skylark, soaring in his own brilliance, he came to mourn both his own capacity for self-destruction and the injustice and cruelty that followed his fall. A *fashionista*, he once had to stand for half an hour at Reading Railway Station in his prison clothes while people stared at him and nudged each other, a shame he never forgot or perhaps even recovered from. Imprisoned for 'gross immorality', he read the New Testament and wrote about what he found.

'Now it seems to me,' he wrote, 'that love of some kind is the only possible explanation of the extraordinary amount of suffering that there is in the world.' [2]

If that was all Oscar Wilde had ever written, it would be enough, because it unlocks the Universe to us.

You can't have pain without love. Or, more strictly, you *can* have pain, but without a context of love it's just the flowing of an electric current down a biological wire, one signal among many for the brain to sort out.

It's only when you baste pain in the sauce of love that pain is truly painful. We start asking questions like, *why me? Why do I get the pain?*

It's almost as if we have a basic expectancy to be loved and for the Universe to be a congenial place. When

---

[2] The quote is from his book *De Profundis*; see my blogpost http://goo.gl/gM7nNt

pain—toothache say—shoves itself into our lives we don't just think, 'Ouch!' or 'Ah! A helpful health update!' We say, 'No!' or 'Not again!' or 'God! Make it stop!'

The biological signal becomes the theological crisis because we expect better treatment. When pain arrives, we are disappointed in the Universe. It, or God we feel, should do better than letting us suffer a twingeing molar. *How dare you let me experience pain? I don't believe in you, but I'm still mad at you.*

Worse still, many types of pain have a random element, which adds injustice to pain. My grandmother and my cousin both died aged 51 of pneumonia. A couple of months ago, aged 51, I caught a severe form of pneumonia called Advanced Respiratory Distress Syndrome, a party animal among pneumonias that kills 70% of the people who host it. I was in a coma for a month, hallucinated entertainingly, and eventually limped alive out of the hospital. I lived. They died. How fair is that?

Another time (I have been in hospital a lot recently), a nurse in the Intensive Care ward at Papworth Hospital in Cambridgeshire told me, 'If this had happened in my old hospital in Scotland we wouldn't have saved you.' Better people than me now lie under Scottish sods while I get to fight, or, well, *type*, another day.

It's a bit random, whether you live or die. But we don't say, 'Fair enough: randomness is part of the Universe.' Instead, we rage at the injustice and look around for someone to blame, suing on Earth and sulking at Heaven. Logic says injustice is part of the created order, but our guts disagree. Life should be OK and everyone should have a fair go, and we ought to be loved. There is a Problem of Pain because we have a built-in expectancy of a kind and reasonable Universe.

Love without pain?

So you can't have pain without a loving context to feel the pain from. Let's ask the reverse question. Can you have love without pain?

I think you can. Or rather, I don't think *we* can, but I think it can be dreamed of.

Take out evil, and take out death and you dig out the roots of pain and only love is left. In a world without evil or death, nothing can hurt you again.

Such a world would be the place we all long for. Seasons would turn, each with new prospects for fun. The world would be ever fresh and new-smelling, but reliably old. Our houses would be comfortable and our neighbours nice. Stretching into eternity, extending everywhere, all we would see would be health, harvests, good days, happy relationships. No parting would be forever. No sorrow or loss would fail to turn out well eventually.

Several thoughts flow from this.

First, love must be greater than pain, because only it can survive without the other.

Second, this mythical, pain-free Universe, eternal, joyful, reminds us of God. It reflects God's Godness better than our current Universe does. Perhaps it is nearer to him.

Third, if it's true that one Universe is so constructed that it has to include both love and pain, but another Universe is theoretically possible with all love and no pain—how come we ended up in the wrong Universe?

4 FALL

So how did we end up in the wrong Universe when all our longing, and perhaps even our true home, is in some other Universe, a perfect one?

The traditional tale, which also happens to be the most powerful idea I've ever met to explain us contradictory humans, is the Fall. We fell from an earlier perfection and the world fell with us. Perhaps we are still falling, going round a loop of fallenness like a computer program that has long stopped responding. We took a tumble from an Ideal. We remember enough of the Ideal to long to get back. But we've crashed so thoroughly we know we never can.

Anthropologists tell us this idea raises its head all over the world. Our ancestors mucked up with God and perfection: we suffer as a result. A West African tribe ceremonially holds its spears horizontally, because its forefathers used to hold them vertically, but they poked God and ruined everything. The Sumerians believed the gods sent a flood, which also ruined everything, because their forefathers were making too much noise.

The classic account of Fall is surely John Milton's epic poem *Paradise Lost*, but that of course is only a stunning poetic riff of his true source: the Book of

Genesis, that ancient, powerful, extraordinary overture in the front of the Bible, just after (in the old Bibles) the toadying dedication to King James of Scotland and England.

This is the great story that has embedded itself into our Western society. Half-forgotten, it still haunts us. Two things have to be said about it.

The first is, it slices us humans open like a trout before a fish knife. Or at least, it seems to explain me pretty well.

Second is, it's completely impossible to believe, when taken literally, unless you stick your fingers in your ears and go 'la la la' to everything else you've ever been taught and to common sense itself. Human fallenness is such a life-changing insight that many good people do indeed do this, preferring this reality to the others on offer, but we need to find a less drastic and less socially awkward option.

It helps a bit to know that the theological rock-stars of the past 2000 years have not taken the early chapters of Genesis literally.[3]

It helps a bit more to think of Genesis using the redolent phrase, 'before theology.'

---

[3] Origen, Basil of Caesarea, Gregory of Nyssa, and Augustine for example. Much later, Thomas Aquinas cautioned against exposing the Bible to ridicule by treating it as a scientific treatise. (See my blog post on David Bentley Hart's book *Atheist Delusions* http://goo.gl/W8V3EB.)

These stories were being told around campfires long before abstract theological discourse had been invented. The first bearded theologian was still to be born long after Genesis's stories had captured hearts and minds. (Obviously, theologians are not born bearded, but you know what I mean. As a species they hadn't evolved yet. They first needed Plato to arise and invent philosophy, and then they were up and running.)

Do you want to know who you are and where you came from? Or what you are, and what you are to do? A story's best. That's what Genesis does, and nothing better is on the market.

It's a story we all think we know, and we think it is about sex, but it isn't. (You could argue it's about good sex and bad sex, for which, for further details, I really urge you to read Milton, but it's honestly not about sex at all.)

In the opening Genesis story, in what must have been an unusually productive week even for God, he creates everything in six days, humans last, with us evidently the cherry on the Belgian Bun, greatest of his works.

We are cosmic dust, but alone of all Creation we are also infused with the life of God. We are made in God's image, which perhaps means we think how he thinks and do what he does, only on a smaller scale. In short, we do what the animals don't do, what evolution would never evolve us to do. And it's all good: the perfect world, all love and no pain.

The Fall comes straight afterwards.

It's important to underline, given that alarmingly large numbers of people in the world are so-called Creationists, to note that the Bible itself is clearly telegraphing at this point, *do not take me literally*. Take me seriously, but not literally.

For example, 'Adam' is a name that no-one else is ever given in the Bible, because it is not a name at all: it's the Hebrew word for 'Human' or 'Humankind'. 'Eve' sounds a bit like 'Living'. The only two trees named in the Garden of Eden are metaphors, not woody perennials: the Tree of Life, and a Tree of the Knowledge of Good and Evil. Apples are not involved. A snake talks and Eve chats with him, rather than jumping a foot in the air and gasping, 'Did you just say something?' Oh, and God wanders about in the garden in the early evenings.

So it's a story of 'Humankind' and his delightful partner 'Living', egged on by a talking snake, eating from the metaphorical Tree of Knowledge of Good and Evil, which—importantly—God said don't eat from.

In a single fateful munch, 'Humankind' and 'Living' freely choose to rebel against God and shun and hide from him.

They only had one thing not to do, strike out in proud independence, but they did it.

At the root of us, teaches Genesis, is a rejection of God and his ways. And an enormous sense of regret.

Thus Adam and Eve are portrayed as first choosing a path that has now been trampled by all humanity's billions of footsteps.

Much then happens. Humans fail to eat of the Tree of Life, despite God having put it in the very centre of the garden as a kind of hint. So Death stalks each of us. By rejecting God and his immediate presence, humans make themselves unfit for the Garden, and they are obliged to leave. They blame each other: not only has the relationship with God fractured, so has their own marriage. Startlingly, around them, the Universe itself morphs into a hard place, with thistles and pain, ruled by that dictator, Death.

Somehow, hardened humans harden Creation; our rebellion, like a bad smell, permeates even the soul and the galaxies and the laws of physics.

When humanity turned from God, Genesis tells us, we lost sight of God's face, became cruel to each other, and took Creation down with us.

But we kept our longings for the Garden. That's why we feel we're in the wrong Universe. We still know the loss and muddle and pain.

The impossible
The Genesis account explains our humanity, pre-figures the dilemmas in every novel that can ever be written, and rings true, but how can it be true? Especially, how can Creation's pain and human fallenness be linked?

Humans came extremely late to the story of the Universe. The first of them would have been born into a world where Death was already reigning, earth was dripping with blood, and thistles and diseases were thriving. The first man or woman would have found no perfect world to be expelled from, even had they stumbled across a metaphorical tree.

Second, and a much bigger problem, is how can such a giant thing as the Universe be somehow entangled with the moral choices of short-lived and tiny beings on a single microscopic planet? Genesis insists the Universe is as it is because of what we humans are. That's silly, or at best completely wrong. Surely we are as we are because the Universe is as it is. The Universe came first and shaped us, not the other way round.

Yes—except when we remember all this is happening under the reign of an infinite, eternal and personality-imbued God, who deeply cares about both people and Creation. If he will pardon the metaphor, he is the elephant in the room. Include him, as he must be included, and the perspectives shift.

Note, for starters, that we humans are more interesting than we think. We have spent the past few hundred years charting our own lack of self-importance in the Universe but this can be overdone, or even completely wrong. For example, stars are simple. Atoms are simple. Even quantum theory is simple, compared with the astonishing complexity of the human being. Maths is enough to describe cosmic expansion or quantum theory; humans require a calculus of their own, one neither Isaac Newton nor anyone else has ever written down.

We are utterly mysterious, when you think about it. Alone, in all the cosmos, so far as we have discovered yet, we are material beings conscious of being ourselves. The only place among all the galaxies where self-awareness happens among arrangements of carbon atoms may be the planet you are sitting on.

I know that other bits of earthly life show the occasional slightly human trait: crows can use tools and whales can talk to each other, and we share 90-something percent of our genes with gorillas, but in every deep thing that makes humanity really human, crows, whales and gorillas are naff and no-hopers. They can't even do reality TV without help. Humans stand alone: perhaps alone in the Universe. Certainly unusual among arrangements of atoms. That's a striking fact.

Or look at it another way. We have already seen that time and size don't matter when you are God. When you are infinite and eternal, the small and the large, the short-lived and the long-lived all look much the same. From where God looks down, a single person can be as important or significant as the whole Universe.

And as we mentioned earlier, when you invite eternity through the door, cause and effect flee out of the window. If human fallenness and creation's brokenness each has a foot in eternity, the problem of which came 'first', or which caused which, goes away. They can be entangled together beyond the reach of time.

Imagine still one further thought. Imagine that we humans are eternal beings. Imagine that somehow we always existed in the mind of God. Imagine that he patiently built the whole Universe so that finally, his good idea could take material form. (It is a respectable theory that the Universe has to be as big as it is, and as old as it is, because it needs that long a run-up to get everything ready for humans to evolve and appear.) Imagine that the Universe is really a kind of scaffolding, to be taken down when finished, replaced with something better, keeping what God wanted all along: friends, beings like him but other than him, enjoying loving relationships together forever in a renewed world.

When you take all that—the uniqueness of humanity, the way eternity and infinity turns the normal calculus to mush, and above all, the fact of God —perhaps it becomes at least possible to imagine that our Universe, ruled by death and lanced with pain, is that way because of the proud moral choices of us little humans.

Which is, like much of my faith, either unthinkable or life-changing.

What fallenness does for us

What does fallenness do to us? It makes us a mixture.

1. It gives us the habit of making unwise choices instead of good ones.

2. It also is the source of a little spring of bad stuff inside: from within, said Jesus much later, out of the

heart, come evil thoughts, sexual immorality, theft, murder, adultery, greed, malice, deceit, lewdness, envy, arrogance and slander. Possibly a few more as well. Most of us learn to hide this stuff behind a civilised mask. But poke us, provoke us, up it all stirs.

3. Yet we remain capable of the most Godlike acts of selflessness, mercy and creativity. There's enough left of the image of God in us that Humanity is awesome sometimes.

4. Each in our own way we long for a better day, for a better world and even seeing it only dimly, will spend our lives working for it. Teaching children, or healing the sick, or building a great business, or helping people thrive or just doing our jobs well: that's what gets many of us out of bed in the morning.

Welcome to fallenness: hurt people and heal people, reject God and strive to be like him. Have Good and Evil jostling together in our hearts and together flowing out into the world, cleaning it and polluting it.

All of humanity, integrated

I can't resist a further question before we leave the Fall. How does it work really? Genesis divides the story into neat scenes, like a play:

1. Perfect world, humans the last and best element

2. Human pride and rebellion against God, freely chosen

3. Fallen world, fallen people.

Cosmology and the fossil record tell us there weren't any neat scenes. There never was a perfect world, a totally free moral choice, and a subsequent crash. Death, for example, was present from the beginning, workhorse of evolution, engine of natural selection.

The only way I can put this together in my head is with a sort of maths. Instead of locating 'Adam' or 'Human' as an individual at the opening ceremony of history, it's better to think of 'Adam' as all of humanity, integrated over all of time.

Perhaps the Genesis story isn't something that happened once, in a past that we all have to now live with. It is each of our stories, put into a blender and swirled together with everyone else's.

Summarize the flickering thoughts, flashing among the whole human species through all of time, the choices between pride against God and surrender to him, between selfishness and care for our neighbour. Aggregate all that, and Genesis pops out. We are Adam and Eve, and our choices are their choices. That is what we have become. That's our story, our nature, and perhaps God's dilemma.

5 THE WRESTLING RING

So far we have worked our way towards a God who exists and who is infinite and eternal in every direction.

Then we have seen how the way humans are, and even maybe the way the Universe is, its pain and joy, its hopes and disappointments, can be untangled by the powerful idea of Fall.

These are our two starting points. In one corner of the wrestling ring, God; in the other, broken Creation and fallen Humanity. What happens next? We can't do much for ourselves (try it: some of us, me included, can't even manage to lose a few pounds, never mind start to deal with a proud heart). All the dynamism and creativity has to come from God. Fortunately, there's a lot of this, because God can be many contradictory things at the same time.

Turbulence

All God's infinite qualities co-exist within himself to an infinite degree all at once. Any turbulence that might exist between God and a truculent humanity is as nothing compared with the internal struggles between God and himself. What happens in the wrestling ring is about the conflicts that must exist within God. And out of these tensions, amazingly, comes the perfect solution.

God must simultaneously hate and love. He must rage against the evil things humans do to each other, whether it's the vast acts of cruelty or the pathetic conceits.

Seeing this perfectly, God must have to sit on his divine hands with all his divine strength in order not to strangle us on the spot. Imagine watching the gas chambers and doing nothing. He cannot feel less than we feel at the rottenness and meanness that goes on under his perfect gaze. He must hate it with all his heart.

Perhaps at the same time he must hurt infinitely too, being, we must suppose, infinitely sensitive. He is infinitely good but is spurned by a humanity who prefer the word of a talking Snake. Fabulous. He gave us one thing not to do, strike off in proud independence, choose blindness over sight, and we all took the bait, and we help ourselves to more of the forbidden fruit every day, addicts all.

Yet he must also love us, yearn for us, want us back. Not to do so would be to be less than God. Nothing is too much bother; he must feel like he would wait for eternity if necessary; but he wants us back.

God must simultaneously want to exert all his almighty power, and at the same time meet us in vulnerability and weakness. A broken Creation and a fallen Humanity must look like an offence to God and his holy perfections.

Like a Father coming home to find a party still going on and the house trashed, God must long to call a halt, throw everyone out, clean up the vomit, take out and burn the rubbish, repaint and rebuild the house. His

Universe should be rocking in tune with his own gloriousness, not be a house of misery. It must cry out to him for a total clean-up. *Roll up your sleeves, God,* he may say to himself, *it's time for this to be* over.

Yet at the same time, if God is really God, wouldn't part of him want to come to the party, stay late, wait till everyone's mellow, join the group sitting on the floor with their backs resting against the wall? Surely he'd decline a joint, but wouldn't he want to wait his turn in the conversation, say his piece? Wouldn't he want to help people home? Wouldn't he endlessly hope that one day a light would come on in the partygoers' lives and they'd realize that happiness is not a multi-pack of supermarket cider? That would be a win, perhaps even a bigger win than throwing everyone out and cleaning up the property.[4]

God must simultaneously want to judge the injustice and take the blame for it himself. Whenever justice isn't done, the Universe tilts a little more from the straight.

So many wrongs in the world, some caused by a broken creation, some caused by what we do to ourselves or to each other. All of us have stories of injustice done to us. Many of us would also admit to doing injustice to others.

---

[4] It's possible to see in these two aspects of God—God the enforcer of righteousness and God the identifier with humanity—the dim outline of what the early church, after much wrangling, identified as God the Father and God the Son. Only one God, but so much of him that you have to resolve him into two faces or two persons to view his depths.

Day after day this injustice builds, and wrong stacks up in the Universe like old pizza boxes, a mountain of justice delayed and denied.

It's in God's power to fix this. He can see everything that everyone has ever done, a long list, and he could, if he wished, issue a perfectly fair punishment to each of us for every offence. We could all be paid back for every act of lazy selfishness or active malice, in some great final Judgement. The Universe, reeling under its load of injustice, would be set right.

There would be surprises. Some of us who thought we were victims of injustice might find ourselves being punished for our resentment and unforgiveness to our oppressors. Some of us who thought we were pretty good might be uncovered as evil-hearted conceits dressed in an urbane or charming face. Some of us who thought we went through life causing little harm might see how many our smugness has hurt.

It might not be Humanity's happiest hour, but no-one could complain. At last, every secret would be revealed, every wrong perfectly and justly punished. No-one got away with anything.

A bigger problem, perhaps, would not be punishing what we have done, but dealing with what we have become. Our individual acts of wrong themselves infect and mutate us. Choosing pride, doing bad, we become worse.

What do you do with eternal beings (if humans are that) who are stuck in a downward spiral, doing bad stuff and becoming worse, evil habits getting ingrained and spreading into the rest of our beings and on into the Universe around us? Eternal beings growing eternally worse? Even here, though, we must assume a perfectly fair and infinitely wise God would know what to do so that Justice was rebuilt.

At the same time, *God must want to take the blame for everything on himself.* None of it is his fault, but why not? he is God. Why not pay everyone's debts for them?

If all the wrongdoing and wrongbeing of the human species can be aggregated together in the story of a single fallen 'Adam', why not come as a second Adam? Why not say, of every act the first Adam did, of everything the first Adam became, *charge it to me?* Blame me, punish me, I'll own it. I created all you guys anyway: how can I leave you now when it's in my power to fix it?

Take everything that's wrong about the human species, the doing and the being, and blame it on me. Leave nothing out. If I come like a Man, and suffer like a Man, it's fair. Because I'm also God, I'll have the power to endure it. Yet because I'm a Man, it'll mean something.

God's mighty urge to do justice for all the victims of the earth can be satisfied by God's equal desire to become a human himself and take all retribution on his own head. Somebody pays—He pays—for everything. The Universe tilts back to the square and straight; and humanity can be free.

The highest peak

We have suddenly arrived at the Christian faith. God simultaneously doer and receiver of justice. God simultaneously Judge and Substitute. He condemns, and becomes the Condemned, so that humans can walk free and a healed Creation can embody love alone. It is magnificent, even for God. Yet anything less would be unworthy of him, because this is the highest peak, and God must scale it.

Christian teaching is that this happened at a moment in history. Around the year 33, about 9:00 one Friday morning, God the Son was nailed alive to a wooden stake, under the motionless gaze of God the Father. God the Son was carrying all the collective sins of Adam. We don't necessarily know how or why but this act became the hinge around which creation's future turned, the engine that powers history.

At that moment of crucifixion we see two hurting faces of God at once. God, Father and Son simultaneously, in love and pain together, unpicking the Fall through justice and mercy.

The cross links God with his broken Creation and a fallen Humanity. It is how, as every genuine Christian tradition agrees, God in the person of his Son died in our place, bearing God's own wrath in God's own human body. God was in Christ reconciling the world to himself. He was doing two things at once: punishing the injustice he so hates; bearing the punishment himself for the humanity he so loves. God the Son, Jesus Christ, became what his cousin John the Baptist predicted he would be, the sacrificial Lamb of God.

The second singularity

Something even more remarkable then naturally unfolded. Three days after God the Son died, having drunk all the poison of rebellious human nature, he strolled out of his tomb.

That day—remembered ever afterwards as the first Easter Day—the sun was perhaps slanting through the graveyard as it rose outside Jerusalem. Nearby, presumably, babies were crying, market stalls were opening, women were collecting water, breakfast was being cooked on a thousand fires, fishermen were cleaning their nets, an ordinary day.

But a few things were not ordinary about that first Easter morning.

1. Jesus had conquered Death. It was gone. Easter Day was death's deathblow. The Last Enemy was conquered by Jesus. It no longer had a hold on him; it had done its worst; now he had a hold on it. It was the end of the line for the end of the line.

2. No-one else had done this. Line up all the prophets, philosophers, religious leaders, holy men, deluded dictators, mad people, saintly people, enormously rich people, escapologists. All died. *All* died. They all stand with us at one side of the grave: Jesus is alone on the other. No-one else ever cast death aside like used wrapping paper. The Christian faith is unique because Jesus Christ is unique.

3. Jesus—God the Son—also kept on being a human being. He didn't vanish in a puff of holy smoke, going back to just being God. Over the next several weeks he strolled along the beach with his disciples, taught them about his kingdom, ate quite a lot of fish. He became, therefore, the pioneer example of a new sort of human being, the beyond-dead sort of human being, the resurrected human being.

4. That day became the starting moment of a new Universe, because the first piece of it wandered onto the scene in the person of Jesus.

5. Jesus was also, and not to be forgotten, having fun. Mary Magdelene, so sad, mistook him for a gardener. I think he wanted to see her face when she realized it was him.

Easter Day was the first morning of a new Universe.

It also showed how New Creation was going to emerge from the Old, how the right Universe was going to supplant the wrong one: through death and resurrection.

Death would de-toxify the old creation; resurrection would be its re-birth. The bad stuff stayed dead; the good stuff, now decontaminated from all the effects of the Fall, would burst out with new life. What Jesus pioneered, humanity itself and the Creation itself would eventually follow: death, resurrection, the Christian hope.

We will see shortly how these truths are meant to change and fulfill the whole direction of our lives.

But first we have to answer another question. *If God is indeed like this, and if he has done this, how does he tell us?*

6 GETTING US TO BELIEVE IT

If you were God, and you wanted to talk to humans, how would you do it? Here are two ways:

1. Send a personalized message to everyone on Earth. This would have to be a 24/7 feed, for the whole history of humanity, to be sure that you captured everyone. People with special needs would have to be provided for. Illiterate people, for example, could not read writing in the sky; deaf people wouldn't hear the audio; and it would have to be simple enough for babies and small children.

2. Send messages to individuals and hope these individuals would be believed by everyone else. (The comedian Woody Allen suggested depositing some money in a Swiss bank account at the same time. It might help.)

Unfortunately, the Fall has shattered our trust in God and magnified our disappointment in ourselves. So the very things needed to hear God are the same things that the Fall has most comprehensively totaled.

Our fallenness makes us ignore God, hide from him, and sometimes bad-mouth him like a former partner from a messy divorce. Some of us find God so repellent that we don't want to talk to him; others of us find ourselves so repellent, or insignificant, that we don't think he'll want to talk to us. Many of us buzz around in our own personal twilight, occasionally smelling some sweet fragrance of eternity perhaps, but never finding the right flower.

Maybe none of these are problems to God, since he is infinitely wise and can solve them, but to us down here, they certainly *feel* like problems.

The communications feed

I think the answer to this communication problem is that God chose both options, and he is now streaming data to us on a lavish scale.

Look at our suggested 24/7 information feed. It's everywhere.

We have seen earlier how the patient work of physicists through the twentieth century led us directly back to a single, joyous moment of Creation. Physics (my subject, though I wasn't very good at it) also tells us other things. For example, if certain physical values such as the strength of gravity were not exactly the size they are (and the required exactness is totally nuts) the Universe would never have got big enough or old enough to host life.

This is true of several other physical constants. It's as if you can twist a camera lens millions of ways but in only one of them is the desired object perfectly in focus. You can try millions of ways of twirling a combination lock, but only one opens the safe. To physics, our

Universe looks very like that focussed-upon object, that opened safe. It's a puzzle, without God.

We also saw that we exist, and that demands an explanation, and we've argued that the best one is an infinite, personal and beautiful Creator. This is a belief with considerable difficulties, but to me more believable than the alternatives.

Beyond those two examples, his word is everywhere, once we look. Creation is sticky with God's paw-prints, scribbled with his crayons, engineered with his genius. Why do babies curl their toes with joy when feeding at the breast? Why are Down's syndrome people so often full of joy? Why is it so *good* to see a field heavy with wheat, or to have a meal with friends, or to share a kiss? Why do scientists find that seeking elegant theories is the best way to unearth the truth? Why are there blue whales or galaxies or the Northern Lights if they don't have a source in God's exuberant joy at being God, overflowing into his Creation?

No-one, not the tiniest baby or the most decayed old mind, or the most handicapped, sense-restricted individual, can escape finding at least a sniff of the glory and goodness of God. We can all pretend it isn't there, but it is. I have felt God's steady presence while hallucinating wildly, coming in and out of a coma. I have known him with me while a crash team was re-starting my heart with powerful electric shocks, at the same time as my body was bouncing across the bed and I was telling the crash team, *that really hurt!*

The more powerless, the more broken-hearted, the more at the end of ourselves we are, it seems to me, the more likely we are to bump unexpectedly into his wordless love and favour. The proud walk straight past him; the broken unexpectedly feel his silent embrace. Isn't it so?

The prophets

I think God also chooses the second method. He speaks to individuals and gets them to teach others.

Now in this world this is a very hazardous thing. We are weary of this stuff. Anyone claiming to be speaking for God is likely to be judged by the rest as either (a) barking up the wrong tree or (b) just plain barking. Part of the reason for this is that the Fall has made us suspicious of each other and of God. But the main reason is that the people speaking on God's behalf can't agree on anything.

For example, God is either passionately for or passionately against gay marriage. He encourages us to douse copies of the Qur'an in petrol and burn them. Or Bibles. Or Salman Rushie's *Satanic Verses*. Afghan women get hit by cars because God requires them to be so covered up that they can't safely see to cross the road. If you don't ceremonially wash past your elbows, your prayers don't count. The earth is flat. The truth is written on a set of golden plates given to the Mormon founder, Joseph Smith, to be read with special glasses, but now both gold and glasses have been lost. Cows are sacred. Or they are just cows. Great wealth is a sign of great blessing. Oh no, it isn't.

What to do with all this stuff, beyond putting our head back under the duvet? How can we distinguish God's voice from among the rest? Are there true prophets? Won't we just endlessly choose the ones that fit our own prejudices?

Our own human judgement is one of the few tools we have in our box. God (if he is indeed speaking within this cacophony) must know that. And my human judgement tells me to look for integrity above all. Show me a truthful person, and I might believe in their truthful message.

Jeremiah's tale

The prophet Jeremiah was a figure in Jewish history as real as others from antiquity such as Cicero or Caesar. He has his own book, more than fifty chapters long in the Bible, and a revered status among prophets.

He plied his prophetic trade at a time when Israel was reduced to a rump state based around Jerusalem and its temple. Empires had come and gone, but the temple ministry had endured for hundreds of years, despite several near-disasters. It seemed like a symbol of God's permanent commitment to the Jewish people. Tradition, history, culture, and the record of previous generations of prophets all agreed.

Jeremiah's message was:

1. Your temple worship is mostly a sham, ritual rather than heart, and you don't care that society is falling apart around you. You're slaughtering the cattle in

the required fashion; but there's no justice in your land. And you're greedy, superstitious and cruel.

2. A new set of invaders is coming, Babylonians, led by King Nebuchadnezzar, and they will invade Jerusalem and burn down your temple.

3. This is a sign that God is fed up with you.

4. Don't fight Nebuchadnezzar. Surrender to him. Let him carry you into exile. Build new lives there. Expect to stay a long time, far from home.

5. Turn back to God.

Jeremiah said much the same thing to the nations around him: *Nebuchadnezzar's coming. You will lose the war. This is happening because of your pride, cruelty and greed.*

Unsurprisingly, he was not a popular figure. He was beaten, put in stocks, imprisoned, and once dropped into an empty water tank and left to die. When this happened, he complained bitterly to God and ranted against his oppressors:

> *Why does the way of the wicked prosper?*
> *Why do all the faithless live at ease?...*
> *Drag them off like sheep to be butchered!* [5]

He was not always totally content in his job:

> *Alas, my mother, that you gave me birth,*

---

[5] Jeremiah 12:1, 3

a man with whom the whole land strives and contends!
I have neither lent nor borrowed, yet everyone curses me. [6]

He had issues with his Employer:

Why is my pain unending
and my wound grievous and incurable?
Will you be to me like a deceptive brook,
like a spring that fails? [7]

Yet he kept to the same message for all his long life. Once the King called him from prison and asked, 'Is there any word from the Lord?' 'Yes,' said Jeremiah, 'You will be handed over to the King of Babylon.' [8] The same King burnt up the scroll on which Jeremiah had written his words, a slice at a time, tossing them into a brazier. Jeremiah's response was to dictate a second edition, and good author that he was, add some all-new material. He was endlessly loyal to a people he (endlessly) insisted were being disloyal to God.

It all came true

Everything came true as Jeremiah foretold. The Babylonians torched the temple and the temple hardware vanished from history, thus spawning a whole literature in the late-twentieth century about the missing Ark of the Covenant.

---

[6] Jeremiah 15:10

[7] Jeremiah 15:18

[8] Jeremiah 37:17

Pleasingly for those who like poetic justice at least, the last King was made to watch his sons being executed, then had his eyes gouged out, and then was exiled to Babylon.

The last we hear of Jeremiah is of him telling the few people left in the land that they should stay there, under Babylonian rule—and then sticking with them as, against his advice, they fled to Egypt.

A new level

Such was Jeremiah's life and message: he received messages from God, backed them with his life, saw them come true. This was a powerful coming-together of personal integrity, prophetic prediction and prophetic fulfilment.

But God did more with Jeremiah even than that.

Before Jeremiah, all the trend in Jewish religion was to centralize worship in Jerusalem. After Jeremiah, the Jewish people had divine permission to settle anywhere, to use a synagogue instead of the Temple, and to re-emphasise that pleasing God is about truth, the heart and the community rather than the ritual burning of sheep-suet.

Thanks to Jeremiah, Judaism could spread around the world. Those of us who are Christians owe our debts to him too: the early church patterned itself on these same synagogues (and often arose through splitting them).

Jeremiah, in other words, in his stubborn and lonely ministry in Jerusalem uprooted an earlier phase of Judaism and planted another one, which then came to serve as a foundation for the rise of Christianity. In a sense he helped make Judaism ready for the coming of Christ. His life of integrity, fused with his prophetic gift, was caught up into God's longer purposes for the Jewish people, and through them for the whole human species.

Now this is what I *call* a prophet:

- a truthful person

- whose words came true

- whose story became part of the larger story of creation, Fall, rescue and redemption.

In the cacophony of voices claiming to speak for God, we have in the end ourselves to decide which voices to choose—if any.

That might mean which holy books to choose, if any. The reason I personally love the Bible so much is that it aggregates so many lives and voices across history and then enfolds them into one dizzying perspective that is actually worthy of God himself—a story that gathers every human and the entire Universe into one coherent account.

It does so through the integrity of its cast of thousands as through the centuries they met God and lived and failed and struggled and died. I know of nothing like it.[9]

And then it invites me to join the story.

---

[9] The Qur'an also claims to be the fulfilment of a larger picture, completing previous Jewish and Christian scriptures, but it can only do so by discrediting them. (See Surah 5 *The Table Spread*, 14-16, for example.) Many of the Christian cults do the same. Mormons claim to believe the Bible but query whether it's been translated properly. Christian Scientists need Mary Baker Eddy's book alongside them so they can see the 'inner spiritual meaning' of the Bible. All these are subtle ways of acknowledging the Bible's cultural force but tacitly shoving it to the sidelines.

7 THE LOSS AND PROPHET ACCOUNT

If God does speak through prophets and if the Bible is their stories collected together, we straightaway come to further problems.

Isn't this book, for example, just a bunch of fairy tales, frequently altered, contradictory; not to mention old-fashioned and even, good grief, not up to 21st century standards of scholarship, general coolness or absence of patriarchal language?

Hmm. It's possible that you may have inadvertently stepped into a pile of dogma.

I find the Bible authentic and robust so long as you understand it as the threaded-together accounts of people meeting God, and God overflowing their language, as he must in every age. Parts of the Bible date back to the Middle Bronze Age. Others are more recent than the golden era of Greek literature. Parts are presented in literary genres that hardly even exist today, such as 'religious history'. Some of it is law code. Parts are sublime. Others, frankly odd.

No text from antiquity comes near it for the quality and range of its sources. Once you stop pretending it is something it isn't, namely a modern book, it emerges like the San Gabriel mountains when the smog around Los

Angeles suddenly clears: massive, daunting, unbelievably near. Until you've read it—seriously read it, like you have to work hard to read any serious book—don't criticise it.

You at least can read it and form your own view. A bigger problem to me is all those who were never able to read it. How is that fair?

Most of the Bible's stories happen among the Jewish people. This is fine if you are Jewish or from a Christian background (which has grown out of Jewish roots). It's especially convenient if you live today and speak English. All the revelation and history is available for you in a variety of helpful formats. Nor are other languages neglected. Christian missionaries and local Christians over the centuries have almost single-handedly put all the world's languages into writing. All except 200m people today enjoy access to at least part of the Bible in a language they can understand.

None of this is much use if your slot in history came and went before the Jewish people even started their sad march across the earth.

Our understanding of pre-history may change, but the view today is that humans just-like-us had already walked from Africa to Australia 40,000 years ago. Perhaps people who are recognizably like people today have been on earth for 50,000 or even 100,000 years.

With a bit of handwaving maths you can guess that means perhaps 100 billion souls have already traced their course through history. The numbers of people on earth today are dwarfed by the number who have gone before:

for every one of us milling about in the streets and filling the shopping centres, another eleven have already lived and died. Perhaps half of these were children or babies.

Nearly all of them were excluded from prophetic words from God.

Even today, plenty of people have access to a Bible but belong to a cultural world that doesn't treasure it, or believes it's been altered, or that teaches people to be suspicious of it.

Can you meet and serve God if you have never heard of him or if you belong to another religious heritage or read another holy book?

If so, how, and if not, why not? How fair is it to be excluded from God's love by being born in the wrong millennium or having the wrong postcode?

It *can't* be true that all religions lead to God, any more than all roads lead to Wolverhampton. [10] They all

---

[10] There *is* a way that all religions can lead to God. This is if the journey is the important thing, not the destination. So 'religion' (or 'spirituality') is like exercise: it doesn't matter what you do, so long as you do something. Some people who believe this like to say, 'I'm spiritual but not religious.'

My hunch is that the destination is important, not just the journey. I wouldn't trust the journey-is-everything philosophy if I was making my lunch. A good outcome to my lunch-making matters: limp sandwiches made with panache are still limp. I feel a philosophy that would lead to unsatisfactory lunches isn't the one on which to hang my eternal destiny.

disagree with each other. They can't even agree on what to fight over. So how can you find and serve God within another religious framework or when your era in history is tens of thousands of years ago?

The non-fairy tale

Near the end of his time on earth, according to the gospel-writer Matthew, Jesus told a story about the Last Judgement. Like all Christ's stories it has passed into cliché and become part of our language. It's a haunting story, almost nursery-rhyme-ish in its brutal simplicity. The early church believed it came from the mouth of Jesus himself, and they would know.

When the Son of Man comes in his glory, and all the angels with him, he will sit on his throne in heavenly glory. All the nations will be gathered before him, and he will separate the people one from another as a shepherd separates the sheep from the goats. He will put the sheep on his right and the goats on his left.

"Then the King will say to those on his right, 'Come, you who are blessed by my Father; take your inheritance, the kingdom prepared for you since the creation of the world. For I was hungry and you gave me something to eat, I was thirsty and you gave me something to drink, I was a stranger and you invited me in, I needed clothes and you clothed me, I was sick and you looked after me, I was in prison and you came to visit me.'

"Then the righteous will answer him, 'Lord, when did we see you hungry and feed you, or thirsty and give you something to drink? When did we see you a stranger and invite you in, or

needing clothes and clothe you? When did we see you sick or in prison and go to visit you?'

"The King will reply, 'I tell you the truth, whatever you did for one of the least of these brothers of mine, you did for me.'

"Then he will say to those on his left, 'Depart from me, you who are cursed, into the eternal fire prepared for the devil and his angels. For I was hungry and you gave me nothing to eat, I was thirsty and you gave me nothing to drink, I was a stranger and you did not invite me in, I needed clothes and you did not clothe me, I was sick and in prison and you did not look after me.'

"They also will answer, 'Lord, when did we see you hungry or thirsty or a stranger or needing clothes or sick or in prison, and did not help you?'

"He will reply, 'I tell you the truth, whatever you did not do for one of the least of these, you did not do for me.'

"Then they will go away to eternal punishment, but the righteous to eternal life." [11]

Presumably Jesus was not kidding when he told this story. Presumably he meant it. Let's note a couple of things:

1. It's universal, about everyone who has ever lived.

---

[11] Matthew 25:31-46

2. The note of surprise. Here, at the end of everything, everyone knows who the King is. They can see him in front of them, revealed at last. Back when they were living their lives, however, they didn't know they were serving him. They may have not known his name.

Pride, humility, selfishness, compassion

The Fall story is about pride toward God. The sheep-and-goats story talks about compassion to people. Are these perhaps two halves of a whole? Does a proud independence toward God also cultivate a certain hardness towards our fellow humans? Does a humility towards God lead to a softness and compassion toward people too?

Perhaps, across the ages, the goats are the people who think they are good and the sheep are those who have discovered they fall short. Actually, goats seem to me to be a lot more resourceful than sheep, though I am not a farmer. Goats climb trees; sheep seem so stupid and panicky, bleating at each other all the time. Generally I'd prefer to be a goat. But perhaps the goats are those who think themselves righteous, and the sheep have come to understand themselves and everyone else as sinners.

This may seem all wrong, but seeing yourself and others as no-hopers and spiritual basket-cases may be a trapdoor into the loving arms of God.

Dirty snowballs

Jesus' story also implies that distance is no object when it comes to the reach of the mercy of God.

It might work like this.

At the very edge of our solar system is a humongous area of thinly-spread rocks, dust, debris, planetoids and dirty snowballs of various dimensions. It's called the Oort cloud. From here, the Sun is barely brighter than any other star. The planets we are familiar with would appear to an Oort object like moths flying near a light, far away.

Every so often, however, the big planets and the Sun align themselves in such a way that an object in the Oort cloud feels a strange tug pulling it sunwards. The other objects don't feel it, because they aren't quite aligned the same way.

But the destiny of this object is fixed. It will leave its colleagues in the Oort cloud, and over thousands of years make its way to the heart of the Solar System, there to enjoy in full the blazing light of the Sun. Pulled by gravity from an impossible distance, the edge of darkness, it might burn hotter than Mercury, or even be consumed in glorious fire.

If the whole of humanity was a solar system with Jesus at the centre, we too would have close-in planets, people who seem unusually favoured in their access to God's words. We would also have an Oort cloud, people very far out, for whom even the name of Christ isn't known, hardly grasping which star to pick as the important one.

It's tempting to see the inner planets as close to God's heart and the Oort cloud as far away. But I don't think that's what Jesus is teaching. People who cannot know his name can perhaps start to have their hearts reshaped by his mercy, and can dimly and distantly start to serve him. The most remote object can be tugged by the burning fire at the centre. It may not move far or fast at first, but it is coming, and God is patient.

Every Christian tradition believes this. That's why people baptise babies. They know that babies don't know what's happening to them. But they also know that God is able to take the tiny, the barely formed, the hardly-started. Then in the context of the eternal nature of God and humans, he is able to bring these barely-formed outsiders from the edge of everything into completeness and wholeness in his blazing light, and in his sweet time.

Even groups that would rather die than baptise babies believe the same thing, though they couch it in different terms. 'Elect' infants, says the austere 1689 Baptist Confession of Faith, even if they die very young, will meet God.[12]

Who moved first?

This of course leads us to an even more difficult question.

Why are some of us proud and resistant to God? Why do others seem to have that resistance broken down

---

[12] 'Elect infants dying in infancy are regenerated and saved by Christ through the Spirit; who worketh when, and where, and how he pleases; so also are all elect persons, who are incapable of being outwardly called by the ministry of the Word.' (Chapter X:3)

so that they are groping towards a humility to God and compassion to people?

Two answers are on offer:

1. Christian tradition and teaching is that ultimately, all the rescuing comes from God. He alone, unaided, gifts forgiveness and extends his arms to us. Nothing we can contribute is good enough. Nothing is needed. God pays the entire bill, bears the whole load, draws us into his heart on his own sweet initiative. It is all his unasked kindness from beginning to end.

2. The ministry of Jesus and the prophets—including the sheep and goats story itself—depends on the idea that we humans have choices and can take the vital decisions and actions about what kind of people we become. In other words, it's up to us.

Who, then, is truly free to act: God or people? Or are both rendered unfree by love? And yet where does love come from if not God? These are unanswerable questions.

The big picture

What we perhaps can see, however, builds together into a picture of how God can be acting across the entire span of human history:

1. He communicates 24/7 with every human who has ever lived, painting with broad stokes his greatness, his beauty, his strength.

2. He sends prophets to fill out the message, so that an informed understanding of him spreads through the world as history unfolds.

3. However exposed you are, or are not, to the messages of these prophets, your heart can be tugged by God without any merit or prompting on your part. Thus even those born tens of thousands of years before Christ can at the end of all things be received into his Kingdom. So can every misshapen, uncategorizable, inconsistent human being ... which is any of us.

8 THE WORLD OF I-THOU

We still can't quite leave the question of how God gets us actually to receive his kindness and forgiveness. I want to suggest a third avenue of knowing, beyond the 24/7 information feed, and extra to the shared story of the prophets that has come down to us as the Bible. It's a dimension of knowing that overflows or even sometimes bypasses our minds.

God does not just care about telling us interesting facts about himself or issuing laws. More than anything, he wants a relationship.

The sort of knowledge he wants to deal in, in other words, is not just 'I-it' knowledge, knowing *something*, such as you could read in Wikipedia. There is some of that, not least the news that he has taken the tab for our wrongdoing and wrongbeing, and we can all start again.

But he also desires what some have called 'I-Thou' knowledge, knowing *someone other*, the kind of intimate sharing that sometimes goes on between a husband and wife or between friends. It is not sharing facts about yourself: it is about sharing yourself.

The problem with 'I-Thou' knowledge is that it's totally different from I-it knowledge. It marches to a different drum. It's fragile, built around two people's feelings and hurts. And it demands humility: you can't just issue it forth from on high. It has to be personal.

One dark day I once said to God, 'I don't want to hear from you. I just want to hold your hand.'

I was desiring I-Thou knowledge more than anything. At that point, I didn't want facts from him or even promises of his goodness. I wanted him, himself. Just to be near. And I think God feels the same way about us.

How does it happen?

So how does I-Thou knowledge happen between us and God? Let's invent a phrase: 'the companionship of prayer.' And let's suggest a third face of God. Not a Father, bearing everything silently on his shoulders. Not a Son, supremely loyal, living a beautiful life of submission. This third face is a Friend, a counsellor, a nudger, an indweller, a strengthener.

Christian tradition of course calls this face the Holy Spirit. 'Holy Spirit' is an improvement on the even older name, 'Holy Ghost', but perhaps it is more meaningful to call him the Holy Friend.

And we straightaway enter a mysterious world, difficult to describe because it's about two beings, ourselves and God the Holy Friend, communicating in total vulnerability. No-one is master here, given that either one of us can walk away.

This is not like the I-It world, where facts are facts, yes is yes, and no, no. Ask, for example, 'does God speak to you?' Now, anyone who claims that God does speak directly to her or him in the I-It world is liable to be locked up in an asylum (or feature on day-time TV, which is much the same thing).

And yet we have argued God desires relationship above everything else. How can you have a relationship if one of the two never talks? [13]

I think the Christian answer to the question, 'does God speak to you?' is 'He doesn't exactly speak, but he doesn't exactly *not* speak either.'

This is what happens in every I-Thou relationship. Perhaps there are times when you speak very directly, and perhaps that is some people's experience of God too. But much more often, you don't need to say all that much. And sometimes you stay quiet even though you could say something. Yet all the time you are communicating, and the thing you are communicating is love in one form or another. In the I-Thou world, it's sometimes more important to communicate love by staying silent than communicating facts by speaking up.

This is where we get to the phrase, 'the companionship of prayer.' It is the place where we talk to God and God doesn't quite exactly speak back, but doesn't quite exactly *not* speak back either. We walk with him, sharing the view. We tell him about our day. We dump our problems on him. We tell him our feelings. We vent our frustrations. We also share our gratitude, perhaps even our songs.

---

[13] My wife might have some interesting observations to make at this point, but fortunately perhaps, this is not her book.

One time in hospital, still quite paralyzed, I had been hoisted onto a commode. I was in a small ward and they had drawn the curtains around me. I had finished on the commode and had pressed the bell for a nurse to come, do the necessaries, and use the big hoist to put me back into bed.

I wasn't in a good place physically or emotionally. English hospital gowns are designed for maximum access and minimal coverage, so I was almost naked. My back hurt. A red rim was forming around my bottom. The smell was rising and filling the ward. I wondered what the three guys on the other side of the curtain were smelling, or thinking. I hoped no-one was serving a meal any time soon. Lunch in the toilet. Yummy.

I did know the guys were each hooked up to their earphones, watching movies or listening to music. In this ward, no-one can hear your bowels burble. Time passed. My back hurt more. The red rim deepened. No nurse came.

I decided to sing a hymn:

It is a thing most wonderful
Almost too wonderful to be
That God's own Son should come from heaven
And die to save a child like me.

I remembered a second verse so I sang that too:

And yet I know that it is true
He came to this poor world below

And wept and mourned and prayed and died
Only because he loved me so.[14]

I sang in a low voice, but with all my heart. Heaven stayed silent, but my spirits were lifted a little bit.

The loose ends

I find the I-Thou world bewildering but essential, maddeningly incomplete but a source of fulness. I have no map to it, I'm not good at it, yet it is always drawing me back.

It's like a walk in the forest at night. I do not know what I am going to bump into or trip over. Yet some of the things I stumble upon are so wonderful. I find that peace can fill my heart even while unanswered questions circle around my mind. Or, for no apparent reason, I can be suddenly flooded with a sense that all will be well. 'Sometimes', said my grandad's favourite hymn, 'a light surprises the Christian while he sings.'

But then, nothing is more naff and iffy and toe-curling than listening to fellow-Christians talking about their experiences in the I-Thou world: 'God said to me...' 'I had a distinct vision of this'. They—I—should shut up. It's embarrassing. Yet I don't think I could have survived hospital without the companionship of prayer. I hate and fear hospitals. Without some I-Thou friendship from God I don't think I could have found the resources to hope. And yet—again—these resources came from a world I cannot find my footing in.

---

[14] William Walsham How (1823-1897) (altered)

The worst moment in the last stay in hospital was probably the night I suddenly started struggling to breathe. The nurses rushed me back through the wards, into units of increasing dependency, finally into the Intensive Care unit itself. They put a big mask called a CPAP over my head, but it was so uncomfortable and I was panicking they had to try others. Finally they found a big plastic bowl attached to what looked like a vacuum cleaner that made me look like Buzz Lightyear but was a considerable help.

My wife Cordelia was with me and on my journey through the wards I thought I had two things I urgently wanted to say to her.

First, I asked her if she could call the prayer team from our church to anoint me with oil and pray for me. There is a Bible reference to this practice.[15] She made a call and a couple very kindly broke off what they were doing that evening, hunted out some olive oil from the pantry, found a car-parking space somehow in the hospital, navigated their way to my bed through the layers of security and hygiene, and duly prayed.

Second, I told Cordelia 'this is not my time.'

I now think that asking the prayer team to come was perhaps a sign of me pulling every emergency rip-cord in sight. But I feel differently about telling my wife I wasn't going to die. She was entitled to take it with a pinch of salt. It's the sort of thing people say in my circumstances

---

[15] James 5:14-15

and then go on to keel over anyway. But I *knew* it wasn't my time, and I urgently wanted to tell her. Once there was a woman who *knew* if she just grasped the edge of Jesus' cloak, she would be healed. She didn't know anything else, she didn't know how she knew, but she knew. And she grasped, hung on, was healed, and Jesus commended her publicly for her faith. From somewhere in the I-Thou world, I *knew* I wasn't going to die. I had the edge of a cloak to hang onto. It wasn't my time.

Later that day they put me into a coma and I was with the fairies for most of the following month, while my wife and family had the emotional route-march of watching the doctors try everything, and then say I probably wasn't going to make it. My temperature climbed to 41.9 degrees. At 42 degrees, I understand, everything falls apart.

But I didn't die. And when I eventually came round, paralyzed and hallucinating, I had that same conviction that I was going to live, properly live again, with Cordelia and my family and my work and wonderful years ahead.

The mystery deepens

Then there is the further, even deeper mystery of people praying for us. From the messages we received, hundreds claimed to be, all over the world. So wonderful and humbling. Yet prayer (at least in the I-it frame of reference) makes no sense. God already knows the problem. When lots of people pray, does God feel somehow trapped and crowded and forced to act? Surely not.

During the worst period of my coma, my church arranged a prayer vigil for us. Different people signed up to pray non-stop over 16 hours, an astonishing act of self-giving and love. Those 16 hours coincided with my temperature peaking, stabilizing, and then beginning to fall.

Six months on, the doctors were kind enough to say my recovery was remarkable. How does that work? I don't know.

It's normal

If any of us thinks any of this is in any way abnormal, we could try reading the Book of Psalms in the Bible slowly, perhaps a Psalm each day for half a year. Then we could venture into the Song of Songs and then perhaps the Book of Job. Between them they are records of people blundering about in the I-Thou world, sometimes bargaining, sometimes pleading, sometimes cursing, sometimes waiting patiently. They are on such an epic scale, and they are all about the companionship of prayer and the I-Thou world.

Some of the psalmists say things to God that I don't think I'd find it possible to say. But then, the people saying these things have suffered as I have never suffered. At least I see through the Psalms that my lesser experiences of God the Holy Friend, in the companionship of prayer, are perhaps at least on the right lines. Surely God is in this place.

The New Jerusalem

One further thing needs to be said about God the Holy Friend and the companionship of prayer. This is how the New Creation is spreading through the Universe.

I have argued that when God the Son rose from the dead, this was the start of New Creation, an event something like the Big Bang, a singularity. Death and the old order was overthrown. God had again stepped into history and done something totally new. There was a new Adam, the first fruits of a new world.

The Bible seems to teach that God the Son's resurrection and then ascension into heaven paved the way for the next new thing in history: the 'giving' or 'sending' or 'pouring out' of the Holy Friend. Soon after Jesus is inaugurated as King in heaven, he unleashes the Holy Friend into the earth. The first stroke of New Creation, the resurrection, is quickly followed in history by another, the giving of the Holy Friend.

The early church was in no doubt that something giant had happened, but they found hard it to put into words. They heard a great wind and saw flames of fire. They were filled with joy and certainty. They talked about the Holy Friend dwelling inside, or of the Holy Spirit uniting with our human spirit. Or they described him as a deposit, the first downpayment of New Creation placed within us. No longer do we have to rely on external inputs to know God, they claimed. Now he is inside us as well.

Two things follow from the pouring out of the Holy Friend onto the earth.

1. God the Holy Friend gives certainty and power to Christians. Christians become (to people who don't share the experience) annoyingly certain that God loves them and they are his children. They continue in this irritating habit even when these Christians happen to be not very nice or good people.

His presence and power, inside Christians, is a new note of hope and victory in the world, evidence that the old order of things is passing away. It isn't like the shadowy days of the remote past, before the first prophets spoke where, as we saw, people weren't excluded from God but were poorly informed.

It's not even like the times when God was speaking to the Jews and the Holy Friend was at work in the world, but only in a limited and patchy way. Indeed the Jewish prophets themselves prophesied about the time when this new and dramatic thing would happen.

'No longer will they teach their neighbour,
   or say to one another, "Know the Lord,"
because they will all know me,
   from the least of them to the greatest',
declares the Lord.[16]

and

'And afterwards,
   I will pour out my Spirit on all people.
Your sons and daughters will prophesy,

---

[16] Jeremiah 31:34

your old men will dream dreams,
your young men will see visions.
Even on my servants, both men and women,
I will pour out my Spirit in those days.
I will show wonders in the heavens
and on the earth,
blood and fire and billows of smoke.' [17]

The early church insisted that with the coming of the Holy Friend, those prophesies were fulfilled.

2. The good news becomes universal. The second thing that came with the coming of the Holy Friend was an explosion. The news of, and the power of the new order of things was sent to the ends of the earth. Famously, Jesus' last command to his people was 'Make disciples of all the nations.' [18]

The church has not succeeded yet in seeing all the nations bow the knee to the new King. But in 2000 years of history, the community of those who at least notionally follow Christ has grown into every country, swallowing empires along the way, surviving every change of epoch.

Knowing, being and doing

Now we can see how God's desire for I-Thou knowing with us changes everything.

Start with Christ installed as the new King in the world, first-fruits of New Creation.

---

[17] Joel 2:28-30

[18] Matthew 28:19

He sends the Holy Friend into the world, somehow dwelling in Christians and—in the context of the companionship of prayer—giving them certainty about Christ's love for them.

This in principle settles the *knowing* and *being* issues that dog us. Our relationship with God, through the companionship of prayer, seems fragile, puzzling and prone to mistake and misunderstanding. We still rebel. Hypocrisy and posing are never far away. Yet we can nevertheless know that God loves us and has adopted us into his family. We can come to a settled certainty about our place in his heart. This is new. It is a taste of New Creation.

Flowing out of the knowing and being comes a *doing*. Whether the world wants it or not, the coming of the Holy Friend carries with it a kind of missionary impulse for the knowledge and power of Christ to be taken to every community and offered to every individual soul on earth. God's desire for intimate knowing of his people sweeps them, like an ardent lover, into his own passion. Which is bringing New Creation into the heart of the old.

Thank you for reading this far

Thank you for reading this far, especially if you don't believe in God.

I know that the atheist description of the world differs radically from what I have given here.

It might go something like how we as a species were not freed by faith in God, but enslaved in dogma and subject to the whims of priests. It might say that we were enslaved that way until Reason and Humanism overthrew it all and set us free. Galileo is often mentioned at this point, then the Crusades, and then probably the way (as I write this) Muslims are blowing up other Muslims in their hundreds for being the wrong sort of Muslim.

I happen to believe this account of the world is a mélange of sloppy definition and over-generalization to confirm pre-existing prejudice. Many better writers have addressed these things, so I won't.

But of course that leaves the question, if the world is as I am describing it and particularly if Christ is King and Lover of it, and if God is here in power as the 'Holy Friend', how can it be in such a state? How can so little have changed over the years? And how can the church, for example, be divided into 45,000 denominations? Why do large parts of it wear silly hats? Why its obsession with money and power? What about all the sex abuse? These are fair questions.

9 THE KING IS AMONG US

Before he left for heaven Jesus promised that he would not leave us as orphans. He had reasons for saying this.

1. He wasn't leaving at all. He was taking up his throne and beginning to reign. He has not gone anywhere, except to reign as King today.

2. He sent the Holy Friend. With him inside us, and with the companionship of prayer available, we can hardly be said to have been left to fly solo.

3. Christ haunts the human species. He's sneaked His way into the Qur'an. Many Hindus worship him (admittedly often alongside others they also call gods). Over the previous two or three centuries, continents have turned to him: Europe has been notionally Christian for more than 1000 years, the Americas for several hundred. Sub-Saharan Africa became majority Christian in the 20th century and in the past 40 years perhaps 100 million Chinese—and rising—have embraced the Christian faith.

4. He told us *how* he was going to work until the human species and the whole earth were ready for harvesting. This explains the world we now see. It also

points up how we can live lovely and meaningful lives, even within the world's now-and-future messy state.

While still on earth, Christ told a set of stories to show what kind of King he was going to be: the parables of the Kingdom. When we look at what he said, it's a bit of a relief, because it explains how the world and the church can be as they are, and King Jesus can still be King, which otherwise might seem very unlikely.

Here are some of the features.

Kingdom things start small. Jesus used pictures of microscopic things like a mustard seed or a grain of yeast that can have huge impact. Given time and a little moisture, a pinch of yeast can create any amount of bread or beer, for example. An oak tree, as it is said, is just a nut that wouldn't give up. Jesus' Kingdom did not start with a continent-wide co-ordinated advertising campaign, but with twelve people, who quickly turned to eleven after one became corrupt.

Yet by the time the Roman emperors started becoming Christians three centuries later, half the Empire was Christian and pagan temples were closing for lack of interest.

So it should be no surprise to us that at any given moment, Kingdom things might look irrelevant and things ranged against them look impregnable. As King, Jesus is happy to start small.

The sound of the pruning shears is never far away. Not only do Kingdom things start small, they are often cut back when they get too big.

Next to the primary school in the small West Yorkshire village where I grew up was a church that could seat hundreds of people. A hundred metres up the road was another one, even larger. The nearby town had several more such hulking wrecks; one of these church buildings has been converted and now claims to be the biggest curry house in the world.[19] I grew up surrounded by vast empty churches.

Charlotte Bronte's novel *Shirley* was set in a grand house near to this same village, and it portrays a world just two centuries in the past but spiritually on a different planet. Neighbours casually discuss theology over a garden fence, for example. That basically never happened when I was growing up.

And unlike two centuries ago, one of the problems the local authorities do not face today, though it happened in *Shirley*, are volatile crowds of unwashed Methodists turning ugly on a church day out. (Today's Methodists, some of them my former Sunday School teachers, would sadly be hard-pressed to form a crowd in the village without bussing in further Methodists from elsewhere. Also, in general, they are more likely to go to a tea shop than turn volatile.)

---

[19] This is the Aakash Indian restaurant, sited, if my memory serves, at the former Providence Place Baptist Chapel.

Even a century later, the Edwardians who built the streets in the nearby town named them after preachers. That doesn't happen today either. My experience is typical, I think: to be English is to live among the lumbering, empty monuments of a much-more Christian-looking past.

This is depressing if you are a Christian, except when we realize it is just Jesus doing what he has been doing throughout the previous 15 centuries or so of English Christianity. It has always ebbed and flowed, been pruned and grown back. A deep cutting-down of the church's size and influence is quite normal, even seasonal.

Slums not state visits. When you become King, you have choices about how you are going to work. You might like to go on state visits and hold high-level summits with other world leaders. Or you may prefer to visit local slums. King Jesus is definitely of the local-slum persuasion. He was that way during his time on earth, seemingly spending disproportionate amounts of time with beggars and lepers, and with the physically and spiritually infirm. His church, to an extent, continues that tradition. It is not surprising that none of this makes the headlines: the quiet and the good don't.

Slow. The work of God's Kingdom, Jesus taught, would be slow, like the 'slow food' movement: seasonal, patient, waiting for things to grow and ripen. You only enter it as a little child. A right heart is given more weight than goals or milestones. It's a power-stripped, vulnerable Kingdom. It's inefficient, spending too much time seeking out one lost sheep rather than simply accepting a 1% wastage in a flock of 100. It finds roles for the infirm and the limited. Not much of this is spectacular. To paraphrase a too-triumphalistic hymn: 'Like a mighty tortoise, moves the church of God; brothers, we are plodding where the saints did plod.' Again, *slow* doesn't make headlines. It just shifts mountains (eventually).

Both good and evil are active forces in our world. In other parables of the Kingdom, Jesus warned that evil would be an active force in our world right to the end. He wouldn't stamp it out early. This is not something we are mentally prepared for. But we need to be, because it helps explain the world.

How did it happen, for example, that two countries such as England and Germany, so similar in history, so intertwined by trade, culture, invention and marriage, came to a point only two generations ago when they were dropping bombs indiscriminately on each other's cities? Evil boiled over is how it happened, a pattern that seems to recur as generations follow each other. No sooner are Nazism and Communism overthrown, along comes Islamism which interestingly attracts the same sort of people who a generation ago were Nazis or Communists.

Why does the Western world in which I am a tax-paying voting citizen and so bear some responsibility, still stop African farmers exporting us their food; sell guns to repressive dictatorships; and run submarines with weapons designed to kill millions of civilians? That would be because evil has been sown among us and we have let it grow.

Does King Jesus approve? I think not. Does he abolish it on the spot? No—possibly because if he did, he would have to abolish *us* at the same time. So an evil world is no proof that Jesus is not King. It is merely proof that King Jesus is patient.

Of course exactly the same principle holds with the Christian church as a whole, which is why criticisms of it miss the mark. Did the church launch the crusades? Certainly. Both oppose and sustain scientific enquiry? Absolutely. Fight both for and against racism and sexism? Exploit and serve the poor? Of course. Will it always be so? Yes—until the harvest.

So, good and evil are both yeasty and active until the end. The continued existence of a bad world and a compromised church doesn't mean God isn't at work in it. It rather means we are all in process together.

It won't get sorted out until the end. Jesus pointed this out often, with different pictures. A netful of fish is dragged to shore, then sorted between the good and bad. A harvest is gathered, then winnowed; the chaff is burnt, the wheat is kept. Sheep and goats will be divided. Up till then, it's a mixture. We need to watch and pray: we can find ourselves on either side. Familiarity with the King is not the same as obedience to him.

All of this points to how Christ's Kingdom can be at work in a world we recognize. The King is among us— really.

And because of that, we can suggest how to live good lives in this mixed-up world.

10 A GOOD LIFE IN A MIXED-UP WORLD

I used to have a friend called Albert, who after wandering for a couple of lonely years through an Alzheimer's-ravaged mind died not so long ago. For much of his life he had been an asbestos salesman. Through the 1960s and 1970s he would kiss his wife in the morning and set out in a succession of 1960s and 1970s cars to sell asbestos to the world. In his spare time he was a preacher and a pianist, and indeed his piano skills stayed with him through much of his Alzheimer's.

In the 1960s and 1970s asbestos was a wonder-material, saving lives by fireproofing rooms, and widely used in the motor industry. Only in the 1970s was it generally understood to cause incurable lung disease. By the end of the 1980s it had become a banned substance and is now expensively removed from buildings by people wearing single-use overalls and respirators, who look like they could decommission chemical weapons in their spare time.

Albert inadvertently gave the best years of his life to selling a deadly carcinogen.

Many of us are like him. Development charities raised funds to drill thousands of wells in Bangladesh.

They didn't know the water was laced with arsenic: the wells saved lives through better sanitation only to then inflict on an estimated 77 million Bangladeshis what the World Health Organization has called 'the largest mass poisoning of a population in history.' [20] It was not an evil dictator who did this: it was charities, funded presumably by the proceeds of a thousand church jumble sales and by people rattling tins in town centres on chilly Saturdays.

Few of us perhaps escape unscathed from wondering if we've wasted our lives. Shortly after I left Intensive Care, my lung doctor found me eating a burger and fries. He could be forgiven for wondering why he had bothered chasing pneumonia out of my system only for me to clog my heart's fuel lines with saturated fat. (But then, he didn't have to eat hospital food.) Surgeons give alcoholics new livers and then watch them take up drinking again. Every political career, famously, ends in disaster.

How do we live a good life?

How do we live a good life?

We live a good life by aligning ourselves with the Kingdom and the King. To unpack a little, we:

Fight the Fall

Improvise

Act in faith, hope and love.

---

[20] See for example http://www.bbc.co.uk/news/10358063, which summarizes a paper in *The Lancet*.

Fight the Fall. We've seen often in this little book the way we all live in the shadow of the Fall. As a species, we've collectively chosen a proud independence from God; as a species, we've been resentful and regretful ever since. We are unhappy divorcees from God, free from him but ruled by Death; proud of choosing our own way but sad to be afflicted and lonely; opting out of his rule but missing out on his love.

There is something heroic about the human species that, even having collectively rejected God, plagued by sin and death, incurable, we fight the Fall on our own. Doctors fight diseases, even though they always lose in the end. Entertainers and artists of every kind fight sadness with hope or humour or inspiration, but the smiles are overwhelmed in the end. Good people live good lives and hope to leave a lasting heritage, but are followed by bad people who spoil it all.

But when we learn that Christ is King and when we surrender to him and his ways, these human instincts are suddenly infused with light and meaning, because Death is no longer on the winning side.

In this perspective, when we fight the Fall, we are serving Christ. Every little win is a sign, an instrument, a foretaste of what's to come. It all matters to a King who connects the present and the future, and the old creation and the new, and who holds everything and everyone in his hands. We fight the Fall for love of him and of our fellow humans and to chalk up a score for the bright future over the tearful present. Why change the soiled bedclothes of a dying patient? Because Christ is King.

Improvise. Christ's parables also teach us that the only way to do good in this world is to improvise. This is because we live in a provisional world.

Once we get used to the idea, it's very freeing. There are only two outcomes for everything I will achieve in my life. Either it will be completely swept away by Death, like a sandcastle in the incoming tide.

Or what survives will be finally revealed as a mixture of good impulses and acts, perhaps, but certainly also soaked in pride and selfishness and much else that reeks of my personal contribution to the Fall. I will have regrets. That's a given. May as well be somewhat reckless in doing good, then.

The call to improvise is to throw ourselves, unabashed, creative, free, using the best of our skills, to serve the Kingdom and the King. This can be in big or small things. Actually, we don't even know what is big or small. We just throw ourselves into what he leads us to—blooming where we're planted.

Act in faith, hope and love. Undergirding it all are three principles: faith (we trust the King), hope (we believe everything we do matters, in the light of eternity)—and love. The Bible is never more eloquent than on this theme. The familiar passage, much hijacked by marrying couples, is really about how life suddenly flames with meaning when you love:

If I speak in the tongues of men or of angels, but do not have love, I am only a resounding gong or a clanging cymbal. If

I have the gift of prophecy and can fathom all mysteries and all knowledge, and if I have a faith that can move mountains, but do not have love, I am nothing. If I give all I possess to the poor and give over my body to hardship that I may boast, but do not have love, I gain nothing.

Love is patient, love is kind. It does not envy, it does not boast, it is not proud. It does not dishonour others, it is not self-seeking, it is not easily angered, it keeps no record of wrongs. Love does not delight in evil but rejoices with the truth. It always protects, always trusts, always hopes, always perseveres.

Love never fails ... When I was a child, I talked like a child, I thought like a child, I reasoned like a child. When I became a man, I put the ways of childhood behind me. For now we see only a reflection as in a mirror; then we shall see face to face. Now I know in part; then I shall know fully, even as I am fully known.

And now these three remain: faith, hope and love. But the greatest of these is love. Follow the way of love... [21]

Did my friend Albert, asbestos salesman to the world, live a good life? I believe he did. The fruit of Albert's whole existence has become a seed, sown now, awaiting the resurrection. He followed the King provisionally, not knowing everything, but trusted him implicitly, served him enthusiastically, believed everything he did mattered. And he loved.

The asbestos will be consumed in flames; the love will glow.

---

[21] 1 Corinthians 13: 1-8,13:11-14:1

11 THE END

Joining this story—taking the forgiveness of God through Christ, and shaking off a dodgy past for a future that is opening out like a rose petal—is easy. Or at least it's easy to say: surrender.

Turn back, give in, capitulate, renounce your proud independent ways, reverse the Fall. Run like chickens back under the wings of Hen Almighty. Fall into the Lover's embrace, close your eyes, smell his hair and let your knees go delightfully weak. You are his, he is yours, for ever and for ever.

This is easy and obvious to understand, but the prouder we are, the harder it is actually to do. Isn't there an exam I could take instead? A payment I could offer? Some great work I could complete? Nope. Just come. We all have to come the same way, stooping through a narrow door. It's easier for children and babies and the small generally: they don't have to duck so far.

Can I retain a little independence, a little of my European cynicism and detachment? No I can't. A surrender is a surrender. I have Adam's choice to make all over again: do I choose to be savvy and self-possessed, wise in my own eyes, or do I choose Life? Do I make and take my own chances or do I just fall into my Father's arms? Do I struggle on, toiling, perhaps using the word 'existential' a lot, or writing dark novels about the meaning of life, or do I give up and give in?

There is the Christ, his shaggy head in outline outside the frosted glass door of my heart. Do I open up, or hide under the table?

His offering to you is more than bananas.

ABOUT THIS BOOK

I have been lucky enough to have been a writer nearly all my working life (since 1983). In 2009 the electrics on my heart started to fail (I was born with a heart condition that made this likely). After a miserable few months, I was admitted to hospital and following an exciting weekend of ventricular tachycardia, alarms going off all night, followed by emergency surgery, I was fitted with a pacemaker—that was my first life.

A couple of years later, the pacemaker lead became detached, and I had a cardiac arrest. My heart was restarted twice while I was still awake, and then several more times until they could stabilize things for emergency surgery. I woke up in a different hospital and now with a second pacemaker lead in my chest—a second life.

Later I discovered that the hospital, the famous Papworth Hospital in Cambridgeshire, served full English breakfasts if you were in Intensive Care and asked nicely.

Then in 2013, I developed a cough which became pneumonia and finally was diagnosed as Advanced Respiratory Distress Syndrome. It may have been related to heart medication I was taking. As I mention in the main text, I was in a coma for two weeks. During that time the doctors took my wife aside and gave her 'the talk'. They had tried everything and didn't have a lot of hope left. Then came the prayer vigil and I started to get better—my third life.

I woke up after a further two weeks totally paralyzed, but that got better too. I was out of hospital by the end of June and walked my daughter down the aisle in early August.

Praise God for the UK's wonderful National Health Service, which gave me all this healing for free, and for the medical staff, who were so smart, compassionate and brave. Family and friends were pretty astonishing too.

These three illnesses, and the long periods of convalescence left me:

More likely to sit for long periods looking out of the window

Less likely to answer emails

More likely to take extended lunch-hours

More determined to write about the things I am really passionate about which in my case is beavering away at the interface between God and doubt, a wonderful and also wonderfully comic place to write from.

During these years I have written two highly unsuccessful comic novels and now this book. Nothing, apart from being part of a family and raising two kids, has been more fulfilling. I couldn't, by the goodness of God, be happier.

More than Bananas started as a convalescent doodle while on holiday in Pembrokeshire, and kind of fell into my lap over the next couple of months.

I sent out more than a hundred Advanced Review Copies and am very grateful for the people who got back to me with comments, many of which saved me from even worse errors than the stuff I've left in. Top among my critics is Cordelia, who rather radically encouraged me to be honest and say what I actually felt. Honourable mentions must also go to Andrew Smith, partner at Deloitte, and Andrew Bowker, publishing director at WEC International, whose comments were particularly brainy and incisive. Old friends Ian and Rachel Copeland took us on holiday to Pembrokeshire and it was so helpful to share with them our two families' parallel experiences of near-death. My wider family were great too. So were many others, too many to mention. My friend and colleague Chris Lawrence created the cover with skill and generosity.

I'm very happy to be in touch further. You can contact me via my website:

www.glennmyers.info

I'm not a huge fan of social networks, but I do have a facebook fanpage. I even do occasional free offers there, but since I am from Yorkshire, and we are careful with our money, I stress the word *occasional*.

FURTHER READING

The following are easily found in various editions on the internet. All are big-selling personal expositions of how the Christian faith works.

G K Chesterton *Orthodoxy*
The best written, most fun and least organized book in this collection, from the eccentric and brilliant Catholic convert.

C S Lewis *Mere Christianity*
The classic exposition from the twentieth-century's foremost Christian apologist, based originally on three series of broadcast talks.

John Stott *Basic Christianity*
John Stott was perhaps the most influential (and certainly the most presentable) leader from the evangelical wing of the church in the 20th century. Both he and his books were popular with students, rigorous and logical.

Tom Wright *Simply Christian*
A giant among academic theologians climbs down from the clouds to the plains of popular theology and offers a fresh telling of the Christian faith in plain English.

BANANAS IN BULK

Bookstores are the best places to go for single copies.

The publisher website:

fizz-books.com

offers discounts for bulk buys and is probably worth visiting if you want to order three or more copies.

PARADISE: A DIVINE COMEDY

You think you've got problems.

My favourite Afghan restaurant closed down. My girlfriend left. A bad-tempered lawyer named Keziah crashed her car into mine. And we couldn't even die properly.

Paradise turned out to be a cage in the heavens where evil spirits market-tested new temptations, where everyone could see our memories, and where we were stuck forever.

A snake with a personality disorder offered us a way out. The trouble was, it meant facing up to the worst problem of all: Myself.

Paradise—a divine comedy is a disorderly romp through death, life, Afghan food and redemption.

Paperback ISBN 978-0-9565010-1-1
Ebook ISBN 978-0-9565010-2-8

Reviews of Paradise

I won this book from the site and absolutely loved it. A hysterical surrealist take on what is out there after life on earth, or next to life on earth, or simultaneous with life on earth, or whatever. A story of Gods in kilts, crystal clear memories, and walls made of our pixelated fears. Delightful. (4 stars) Jeannette M, Goodreads

I also won Paradise in the goodreads competition…and I am really glad that I did. I didn't love the first chapter since it threw a bit too much weird at you all at once (penguins which pull your soul around are an example). After that, the story got going and was really enjoyable! Sometimes you want to hit the main character on the back of the head and tell him to stop being a wuss, but how would you react if you had to build a paradise controlled by some used-car-salesman-style gods? If you like quirky and surreal stories about the afterlife, then I would highly recommend Paradise. (4 stars) Katie Webb, Goodreads

A superb rollercoaster of a story; loved every minute! Phil Groom of the Christian Bookshops Blog

So hilariously funny! I've already started reading the next one. I would highly recommend this to just about anyone. ' (five stars) Stewartc85 on Goodreads

Myers is a great writer and his style is terrific… this was a great book Martin Gibbs Amazon.com, Goodreads.

What a great book! Loved the characters, the creativity, the dialogue, the imaginative idea of evil spirits keeping humans as pets, the insightful lines: 'a creative, radical thinker, but not a creative, radical doer', for one example; the image of the rain of God's mercy, …. There is much to think about beyond the story itself and the book gives a delightfully comic but definitely insightful look into the human psyche and soul. It's a mark of a good book (for me, at least) when I look forward to picking it up again to read and am slow to put it down. I loved every aspect of it. I was given Paradise by a friend who knows I enjoy good lwriting. I have to say that any book which keeps me reading the next chapter because I've become absorbed in the characters and the unfolding story is a book well worth reading. This is one of those books. I look forward to the sequel. (4 stars) S Sutton, Amazon.com

Loved the plot, the characters, the dialogue, the pace, the suspense, the surprises, the imagery, the metaphors, the depth, and the meaning. And I laughed a lot. It is really wonderful. Kenny Parker, Amazon.co.uk

THE WHEELS OF THE WORLD

Thanks to a near-death experience, Jamie Smith can commute between earth and the heavens, where souls swim, ideas grow and improbable dollops of joy fall through the sky.

Jamie and his scary colleague Keziah have been recruited into an eccentric organization that tries to fix broken souls and change the course of history. Which is fine, except Jamie isn't too sure about the health of his own soul—and definitely doesn't want to find out.

He'd rather be working for The Department, the heavenly bureaucracy that plans the future universe and offers a 30-hour working week, enviable employee benefits, and a tennis-skirted line manager named Anna-Natasha.

As Jamie's problems mount, dark forces close in, and time runs out, he's left with a decision: if he's fleeing from himself, which way should he run?

The Wheels of the World, sequel to *Paradise: a divine comedy* is a comedy about how we change on the inside.

Paperback ISBN 978-0-9565010-0-4
Ebook ISBN 978-1-4523-8994-3

Lightning Source UK Ltd.
Milton Keynes UK
UKOW06f2141290416

273250UK00006B/64/P